LOVE'S AUTOBIOGRAPHY: THE ENDS OF LOVE

selections from 'The Many Loves of Duane Vorhees'

LOVE'S AUTOBIOGRAPHY: THE ENDS OF LOVE

selections from 'The Many Loves of Duane Vorhees'

Duane Vorhees

Hawakal Publishers

Published by Hawakal Publishers, 185 Kali Temple Road,
Nimta, Kolkata 700049

Email: info@hawakal.com

Website: www.hawakal.com

First edition (India): July, 2018
Copyright © Duane Vorhees
Cover designed by Bitan Chakraborty

ISBN: 978-93-87883-17-8 (Paperback)

Price: INR 250
US Dollar 8.99

CONTENTS

PROLOGUE

BETH

JENNY

YEOBO

EITHER ALZHEIMER'S OR THE LIGHTNING BOLT

Whizdizzyingly
cruising The Moment,
arrowing past all awareness:
highway, enginewhiine,
steeringwheeltrafficWorldsmudginnnnngg past
while we, preoccupied, reprise Creation,
absorb Eternity and Logos, Eden/Gethsemane, Genesis-
Apocalypse
and the Night the Night,
the private bleeding into the general,
and Ouruniverse proxying for ego.
Glorious cosmic fusion in an infinite minute. (or so it
briefly eternally seems in our infinitiny microverse)

The ends of love
are but two

:your V8 plunges from the surface
and, crucified like a butterfly in time,
helpless consciousness heightened,
you hover in slow motion witness
to the juggernaut earth's decay
just as your metal-again grille
begins to embrace solidity

or: doomed foresight eludes
as you rear end that lightless
semi-

7

ANOTHER SPRING NIGHT IN FARMERSVILLE, OHO

The sun is a gong hung low across the sky.
windswept. earthdirty. sunwhipped: farmers wait inside
their bones
for the horizon to rise and beat the daylights out of the
sun
and call them from their long dungrows for a night.

Your chastity's a song sung slow through long nights
on muffled virginals: muting babies wailing to be born:
baiting the summons of some greedclad huntsman with
silver horn,
golden arrows, a thong-strung bow.   *the dream knight.*
The night is calling: strong, gung-ho—black hawk in flight.

*(tonight? When one earthtired husbandman works me in his hands
& periods this dry chaste day, waters these furrows hungry from
famine?*

But no.
          Just one more wrongtongued crow in flight.)

8

AH! NIGHTS

Ah! Nights you were a harem
and I the unmade Bedouin too long in the thirst.
Past the black eunuch of the night
I would steal to your tent,
unarmed save one single arrow in my quiver.
I'd draw sensuously back your damascene veil
and let fly my shaft
deep into your bull's-eye arabesque—

Or: you were queen of the hive
and I a drone among the honeys
getting a buzz on and doing my job
plunging among the dusky clover
trying to pollinate the skies
to flower the night with stars.
To lose my only stinger would be to die—

Or else you were Madonna
awaiting your Jealous Commanding God,
The Spawner Of The Cosmos,
Beam Of Light Made Flesh To Hold You In Your Place
(while you shook in rapture for the coming of your Lord,
i a small choirboy would steal into your unguarded
churchyard and send a solitary firework into the
cathedral's secret hole and hope it explodes high up in
those beribbéd vaults and surprise celibate fathers from
their sleep).

FRANCIS DRAKE

My hands are caked and yours are so fine,
but somehow they fit
trim together like ships of the line.
Marry me, oh carry me, sign your name mine:
I'll be Francis Drake and you'll be my Golden Hind.
I'll fill up your hold with all of the gold
that I can find, all of the gold that I can find.

We'll dance naked, if you're so inclined—
just billow our charms,
wrap our sheets round yardarms entwined.
I'll ride you oh I'll guide you, make your name shine.
I'll be Francis Drake and you'll be my Golden Hind.
I'll fill up your hold with all of the gold that I can find,
I'll fill up your hold with all of the gold,
with all of the gold,
with all of the gold
that I can find.

I'll be Francis Drake and you'll be my Golden Hind.

MY FINGERS

Visit me in my mushroom tower and I will come to you
down this deep dark ditch amid tinder black flowers
down to the buttercups and dew.
My fingers have ridden through the forests of your hair
and slept on belly-gold prairies.
They've explored your hidden valleys, climbed
snowcapped breasts,
and on your beach hips have rested.
Tanned and naked you are, strata in the earth in layers of
dark
light
dark
light
dark;
while (miners in anticipation) my fingers tremble....

And then it is we who are the layers in the dark, quaking
among bedrock,
hardness melting into darkness, joining in new formations,
stalactite buried and unearthed buried unearthed buried
unearthed
through the long geologeons of night

till finally separated by a fault

...and our sky becomes snow on coal.

WITHOUT YOU BETH
MY LIFE

Beth:
I miss you often.
These paths unmapped and all my everythings nones,

(near me still your spirit hovers
but — unattached!)

standards weighed by a crooked butcher's variable pound.

*

Breaths used to lift dolphin-like
from our depths
like frost balloons toward the sun

in/and/out, those breaths of lovers
with joys unmatched.
up/and/down/and/up/
an ocean-rhythmed merry-go-round.

*

Death.
Abyss-dropped coffin.
Everyone wept. Someone mumbled a little Donne.
Then they handed round the shovels.

(An egg unhatched:
without you Beth my life's another burial ground.)

*

Faith?
My fists clasp-softened, fingernails ripped—
faith, you say?
A black-habit nun who whispers yes but means never.
Faith's record's scratched:
Here's how a faith radio with no aerial sounds:

JENNIFER IN TWO VOICES

I know why the sky sings the blues — for you, Jenny, for you – atmosphere breaks down and cries. Once the wind must have had your voice: Wind makes my soul rejoice to hear you echo once more. Your precious beauty to preserve, earth freezes to its nerves in ecstasies of ermine. And the waves for you outreach — the sea begs up the beach, hands-&-knees its way in pride. And trees have honored you in gold, red carpet where you rode, jade ceilings and emerald floors — nature's learned your lesson well how to be beautiful: your appearance is your sermon.

I know why the sky sings the blues – for you, Jenny, for you – atmosphere breaks down and cries. (*Across the landscape many-firred, atmosphere breaks down and cries,*) Once the wind must have had your voice: Wind makes my soul rejoice to hear you echo once more. (*urges us make love manifold. To hear your echo once more*) Your precious beauty to preserve, earth freezes to its nerves in ecstasies of ermine. (*among the creeks and conifers in ecstacies of ermine,*) And the waves for you outreach — the sea begs up the beach, hands-&-knees its way in pride. (*in fields of foxes henna-furred — I hands-n-knees my way inside*) And trees have honored you in gold, red carpet where you rode, jade ceilings and emerald floors — (*where moist warmth is plentiful. On jade ceilings & emerald floors,*) nature's learned your lesson well how to be beautiful: your appearance is your sermon. (*raven-eyed/ lynx-face Jennifer: Your appearance is your sermon.*)

Across the landscape many-firred, atmosphere breaks down and cries, urges us make love manifold. To hear your echo once more among the creeks and conifers in ecstasies of ermine, in fields of foxes henna-furred – I hand-n-knees my way inside where moist warmth is plentiful. On jade ceilings & emerald floors, raven-eyed/lynx-face Jennifer: Your appearance is your sermon.

"MUSHROOMING"

If you were forest
I could purport
this noble purpose
for these frequent
meticulous surveys
that I perform
throughout your moist
and fetid shadows.

sAVAnnA

AblAze WiTh hUnger/discovery
,epiderM AnTs rUn eleCtriC AgAinsT This plAin:
ThrOUgh YOUr CUrlY grAsses These sOfT YellOw
liOns
prObe   And Under The ripe VUlTUres in The
briArTrees
MY YOUng ChiMps rOMp UpOn gOlden MOUnds—

O The Wind glows WiTh dUsT & dArK MYsTerY

And O The MOOn hOWls
        AbOVe
            Us. And YOUr riVer sWAllOWs mY
            AArdVArK.

ATOLL

Poets before me (how many) have extolled
:melons full melons ripe
:those raspberries (pink & wrinkled) delicate atop your
double-dip vanilla sundae
:your slice of peach:your wedge of pie :your pyramid of
hot cobbler,
tart sweet juices oozing like fresh tar on the newly laid I-
in August Texas. . .

but none has ever praised
:the gold and graceful arc of the taut banana—
O huntsman's bow before release—
:the strong sweeping scimitar of a Southern Cross bole,
bent fullsail,
fruitful coconuts proud unfurled,
or :the sweet white sticky elixir inside. . .

no one has ever
noted for eternity
the coy Thanksgiving yam.

MONTANA MOTEL
[and the radio cowboy sings]

Come lay your body down close next to mine.
Sure, yes I'm sure, your husband won't mind.
We're in Montana, and he's in Japan.
So lay your body down. Lay it close next to mine.
Just turn your lamp off, and close down the blinds.
If he came home to find us entwined,
Your husband's a good man, he'd understand.
So lay your body down. Lay it close next to mine.
(asleep beneath the bower of other tresses,
I do miss the slow flower of your eyes.
But I'll water I guess the garden of her yeses
till I rest in the hollow of your thighs:
Is what we learn worth the loss of what we forget?)
Come lay your body down close next to mine.
Sure, yes I'm sure, your husband won't mind.

Sure, yes I'm sure, your husband won't mind.
Sure, yes I'm sure. . . Sure, yes I'm sure. . .
(though I taste the desserts of another's mess,
I still miss the silvered service of your limbs.
I must suppress the appetite of these whims
till again I can dine at the table of your breasts.
Who else turns his face from the light to stare at shadows?

Who abandons the concert to attend to echoes?)
Come lie here beside me, pass down the wine.
Sure I am that your husband won't mind:
Needs in Montana can't wait for Japan.
So lay your body down,

19

Lay your body down, body down. Body next to mine. . .

QUEEN OF DENIAL

So Jennifer you are.
Wrapped in just your thoughts, (and mine too) (*not that
you'd notice*) you assume the Mummy pose in bed. Are you
sure your heart's hermetic, secure in its canopic jar? Or is
it yet in your breast, just beyond sight, cowering still?
(And don't forget your nightly negative confession—the
world's bad deeds you've never done—
all of them—don't miss even one.)

And that kind woman in the Registry told you, didn't she,
as kindly as she kindly could (but in the blameless guilt of
your secret vacuum heart, what was it you heard? And
how in your soul did it reverberate?) "*Sorry.* This is all we
have. This is all the information anyone has. We can't find
out *who you are*. We don't know what year you were born.
We can't find out where you were born. Nobody knows
who your parents are, your mother or your father, or why *they
didn't want you*. Someone—we don't know who—found
you, wrapped in a *ragged, dirty* blanket, lying by the side of
the road. You were turned over to the authorities and you
were sent to the orphanage. And that's all we know. *I'm
sorry*. I wish we could help you. *Sorry.*" Of course, you
knew the whole story already – how could it hurt you
now? "Don't touch me," you warned me as kindly as you
can manage. "If you just leave me alone [*you, too!*] I can
handle this by myself."

But: a single slow tear somehow engineered its hopeless
escape down your Alcatraz cheek.

Wrapped like a glove on the dresser. Lovely warm soft leather. Carefully crafted. Turned nicely out. Waiting for the proper hand.

Together *(does that word really mean separately alone?)* in bed again.
Pickets intent, rapt in their mission, inspecting invisible perimeters.
    "All lines secure, Sir."
No intruder can penetrate.   *(friendly, or otherwise)*   And there you lie, wrapped around your arms   (not my arms), world-weary frightened.

So, Duane you are.

FOR LOVE

You wanted to share my life;
time kept you from my past; the future hasn't come yet;
today is just for laughs.
Sometimes I know I bored you,
and other times ignored you.
You know how I felt toward you.
But to say I wanted no one but you would not be true.
I auditioned my actors, and you weren't in the cast.
Fitting out my clipper life replaced you with a mast.
You know that I adored you.
But once I had explored you,
I just could not afford you.
Many a man has decayed and gone to bugs—but not for
love.

THE BEAST

And now who's going to drool at your beauty?
Who's going to bark through the night?
Who's going to bury
his bone for you today?
and howl for your exclusive delight?

My head has become a slow white dove—
no match, I'm afraid,
for the swiftsweet addresss of your fingerssss.
and
already
Just a flikflik of the tongue,
one whiplash embrace –
and
already
the rich delicious poison
invades my heart.
And now who's going to drool at your beauty?

Who's going to bark through the night?
Who's going to bury his bone for you today?
and howl for your exclusive delight?

Imagine our bodies in Braille,
finger tongues perusing,
teasing out nuances,
weighing every significance.
We turn over
sheet after sheet.

Each climax foreshadowed,
we read ourselves to sleep.

And now
who's going to drool at your beauty?
Who's going to bark
through the night?
Who's going to bury
his bone for you today? And howl for your exclusive
delight?
I love your body's several smiles
as I press my name on all your mouths.
I love the way your body smiles
in some of your most surprising places.
I love the several smiles your body hides.
I love the hidden ways your body smiles for me.
The Easter Egg Hunt of your passion. The gift at your
Christmas tree.

And now who's going
to drool at your beauty?
Who's going
to bark through the night?
Who's going
to bury
his bone for you today?
and howl
for your exclusive delight?

No music's only one finger on one string.
The ocean wants a moon to make a tide.

Left foot needs right to create a stride.
And flight requires flow and wing.
It all makes a kind of bawdy sense:
Selfish soliloquy, no audience.

And now who's
going to drool at your beauty? Who's
going to bark through the night? Who's
going to bury his bone for you today?
who howl for your exclusive delight?

sticky nights
with a peppermintcheeked wonderchild
gumdrop breasts and licorice thighs
and acres of sugar cube smile
(even sweets will turn sour
if left for overnight;
too many lonely long hours
between the passion and delight)

And now who's going to drool at your beauty?
Who's going to bark through the night?
Who's going to bury
his bone for you today?
and howl for your exclusive delight?

I've had my wine.
my kiss and my cock,
my garden and my trial.

I've got my thorns,
my thief and my hill,
my boulder and my style.
Where are my ring,

my fief and my rod,
my halo and my choir?

HER NAME IS JENNY AND MANY A MORN HAS WORN HER FACE

:daybreaks are harlots all scarlet and huge with rouge and paste.
:some skies all rosy with hosiery (her limbs so prim, so chaste!).
:some days hemorrhage like courage at our battle place.
:other sunrises are sizes too small — whole yards of lace:
silk towns are pretty, but cities of silk go wilt and waste.
(So like my Jenny: her any is much; her touch, embrace.)
(There is no middle. A little with her will work long ways.)

:brown coffee mornings come pouring right up from cup to taste.
:all these sun risings (dawn-icings) — like thieves, they leave no trace.
(So unlike Jenny:
so many a morn has worn her face, so many evenings.
Her leaving goes dim with flimsy haste.)

STILL STRANGERS (Prologue)

After years
   of wear, she would sew,
with those sharp dead
           beads, new thoughts
       into the threadbare pattern of memory
and he solder
   his, older, thoughts into place. . .

                  ...Long ago...
they learned to slaughter
   their eager laughter and tear
      their deepest tears out of each other,
      to utilize their exquisite words
    like hamhamhammers and broadswords—
   then, their mutual wounds
       they wound all about their lives like
poison ivy.
(Each just one more bothersome
     clone to the other. . .)

But.

There had been a time
   ,once,
      before the tiny
       mutiny,
when they were still strangers
       to anger;
when they could lie sun-baked
       naked upon the Jurassic sands

or beside the slow hearth
                    unearthing new treasures from their
together,
when,
            in some safe
                café, their yes
                        -eyes could swallow entire
        their sweet menus
                of Venus
and for many an hour
                pour their love
from lip to mouth like milk from a pitcher to a glass.

                            But that time passed...

VOLCANO

Now dawn. When this
grayed well-done sky
resumes to rare.

And—sudden flare!
awakes this wife's
night-dormant kiss.

SOLSTICES
(after *Hwang Jini*)

Take one half the night
of the shortest winter day
and wrap it in your arms,
a prudent negligee
to unfold one brief summer night
when you hold me in your arms.

THIS IS HOW IT ALL BEGINS

Mother Sky Aphrodite
slides into her nightie
(Silk. Black. Strobe-filled sequins.)
and glides like Ponds into bed.

Papa Earth rolls over once,
hugs her, humps her, then grunts,
groans, snores, snorts; sprawls like lead.

From their bedclothes crawls a Moon-faced
offspring, squalling till the dawn,

when a newer, brighter son
spits up in his spoon.

A POEM WITH A TITLE NEAR THE MIDDLE

felt hammer
     a stammer

/a sermon

honey in an
      iron jar

  a temple/
a jungle

(:Marriage Is:)

philosophy
    and football

"YES, BUT WHERE ARE THE WHEELS?"
    --Albert Einstein, at 2, when presented with a sister

—What is woman? A boon-&-hex, sometime-mate /
sometime-check
—Oh, what's man? An egg-ego? A comic book hero?
—A brain with bones.
—Mixed with chromosomes!
—Woman is the ultimate X.
—The Royal Comptrollers of Sex, we're architect-builders
of children, passion's pilgrims.
—Man: atoms with kinetic glands, machines-with-hands.
—An electric orangutan!
—You Singer-Device, all undone. Man's the Iron Cross
and the iron dream.
—An iron sculpture of sweat and jizzum.
—A puzzled philosopher's tired scream: Why can't women
be a syllogism?

DON'T GET ME WRONG

Despite all these eons of together, you still want me to
write you poems? Okay:
"the stars: scattershot across the purple night / like bird
shit on velvet"
Don't like it? Terribly sorry. This lack of sweet poetry, can
you forgive?

But beyond your vertical crescent smile
there lurks O swastika – Mona Lisa skinners box.

When you sleep your closed eyes look like tiny Chinese
twats.

Though your eyes no longer burn with magic
and this hour with infinite possibilities won't swell any
more,
yet your quotidian eyes still warm the frosty air,
and I don't mind my time with you.
And your arms don't anchor my lusts as they did before,
and your form isn't the amusement park it used to be
when I was the new ride,
but your embrace remains a comforter in the cold winter
nights
and the scenery's quite nice still.

TAKE ME IN

"Take me in," the poet said, "take me in." The prophet
hid.
"Take me in," the poet prayed, "take me in."
No banker paid. "Take me in." The soldier fled.
"Sink or swim," the lawyer pled. "Take me in,"
the poet said, "take me in."
A woman did.

"Make me warm," the woman cried, "safe and warm."
The poet sighed. "Words are thin," he did reply, "weak
and thin.
But yet I'll try. Weak and thin, but yet I'll try."

In the bin by page by page,
in the bin the books were laid,
inch by inch were set ablaze.
Line by line the match was lit.
Word by word
the poems all went.

"Now I'm warm," the woman said,
"safe from harm. But poet's dead."

Poet dead?
Poet dead?
He lives on inside her head.
Words go on inside her head.

A POEM AND AFTER 60 YEARS A REPLY

Lying

Knock, knock, knock,
please open the door
let me stay the night
 It's late and it's cold
 Who can it be?
I opened the door
and saw the tail of a black dog
lying.

Cluck, cluck,
laid an egg
Here girl come and get it.
 The girl ran to see
 the egg oh the egg
it was only an insolent hen
caught in broad daylight
lying.

  — Yun Dongju, 1937

Lying

Canine, chicken
live next door
in annual menageries,
 Dog on tiger: okay.
 Hen and tiger too.
Why not rat on rat?

38

Manual for interspecies mating
lying.

Doak-doak, Doak-doak
five zodiac-dozen cycles
makes us a sage.
    The man and his tele-V
        grew gray waiting,
got wise and up after 60 years.
All calendar's fault
lying.

CONTRETEMPS

The tense contentment of the nights before
now in contempt
gives way to temptation.

BUSSES AND CROSSES

[blues]
Life deserves a measured look.
Life deserves a measured look.

[country]
I had a dog but dog ran away.
I had a girl and the girl did stay.
I had a dog but dog ran away.
I had a girl and the girl did stay.

[blues]
Plusses and losses shape our plans.
Plusses and losses shape our plans.

[country]
Girl, she sears my nights
When snow chills the ground.
That girl fries my nights
When snow is on the ground.

[blues]
Life is like a ledger book.
Life is like a ledger book.

[country]
Girl, she sears my nights
When snow is all around.
But summer days
I still miss that hound.

[blues]
Busses and crosses map our lands.
Plusses and losses shape our plans.
Life is like a ledger book.
Life deserves a second look.

LEAP FROG

In slo/
   /mo,

                             /frog,
             tree, and, shade, leap/
Seasons pass, and Velcro lovers to Teflon stray.
Tomorrow
will we kids too play,
  kids
  play   leap
                 frog
                   leap?

EVIDENCE FOR THE MUTATIONAL CODEPENDENCE OF TIME

Yesterday
today
was
tomorrow.
& my future

:ours.

WHAT WANTON

Which village chemist took us from his shelf
and mixed us with his pestle,
          put us in pots,
and sold us to customers with their milk?
(they took us with cereal
          and died in knots)

And which astrologer played with ourselves
his odd game of celestial
          connect-the-dots?
(he made the moon turn the tides into whales
against glittery crystal
          chandelier yachts.)

DOWSER

Once I was proudly regarded
as the foremost geographer of You:
I surveyed the careful topography
as I mapped your features anew,
measured each promontory encountered,
and charted every defile.

Many times had I plumbed for your treasures
and glad had continued my earthy research.
And I knew I could move
my stretched willow out
to discover the sweet waters below.

But now that I live in exile from You,
now that your landscape has gone,
I find it was not your true geomancy I'd learned.
For though I'm sure that it was your well I discerned,
I never divined the source.

ONCE, ONCE

At one time some people believed
that the elephants
had sex but once:
No wonder such a memory!

Once, I thought love was measured
in some mean distance of imaginary numbers
from whole digits to infinity squared.
One perfect combination. (*The tumblers
turn and twist.*) My sandpapered fingers
bared to the wrist. But secrets hide
      in the between.

Once, love was obvious as the ebb and
flow of ocean is to charts and sailors.
(But sea, O sea – you scene of unseen
sights – you graveyard of mariners –
a gale, a new leak, or a sleeping watch,
and your white wave just swallowed me like bread
      unleavened.)

Does a lemming really embrace the sea
with a lover's greed?
To know the sea, roughly
one taste's enough.
              But what about love?

TRAD

So we pooled together our quarters
to buy a beige wedding dress
and hire a birdsong processional
and a greenwood wedding hall.
Deciding to forego a sermon,
we said those words that we meant,
and we solidified everything
with wine kisses and smoke rings.
But then this mud ball rolled below us
and moved us separate ways.

WORD

I started this work in cuneiform
but I couldn't undam the poem.
The stone wedged it. Bereft, mute, tuneless,
the task I adjourned to papyrus.
The flooding rendered it all a smudge,
its squiggly hieroglyphic unedged.

I converted to parchment and quill,
betook myself to tonsure and cowl,
to abstinence and flagellation,
but manuscript illumination
of my holy writ couldn't complete.

Printing press further repressed my wit.
O! Its backwardness and reverses
transformed my tersests into curses.
Typing required guitarist fingers,
not these mallet hands of my nature.

Word processors came to my rescue
at last! Too late, alas, for my muse.

THAT Y IN MISER IS ME: A MELODRAMA

I had thought to hoard your beauty,
to store it safe and proud
in that place where you'd amused me
and none else would be allowed.
But you crept out through the tower,
and you burst out into World.

Now you perfume your universe
with circus, peacocks, clouds. . . .
while I stay locked in duty
with my memory and my

                        (*shroud*

    almost I wrote. A miser's booty
    lost!!! Hyperbole for the horde.)

EROS IN
EROSION (Epilogue)

Strangely
    angel-like, two
naïf
waifs
blown
down.
        Unable to unwind all the ivy accumulation
            in a rugged wind they just
                shrugged, unable to adjust,
                    unable to face down
        the demons of their facetious selves.

            (This is not simply
                        to imply that they weren't determined.
            But, over time, stubborn assiduity becomes undermined,
            especially when connubial cement lacks
                            reinforcement.   So,
            by fragile grapevines, over
                tangled ravines, the values they were hanging onto
                                kept changing:
            unable to forge a structure anew
                or to forget old collapse.
            And neither the heights of their dear science nor
                        the weight of alerted conscience,
                and not Keats and certainly not
                        Yeats,
                    could keep the crevices in their isolate selves
            from inventing the devices of their together's undoing.)

51

Beached,
    they discovered the sea:
        inequal parts nausea and mystery.

HAWKED AND DOVES

Love is hawked from every ad,
is sent likes doves from all our arks,
is aimed at every easy mark,
is scribbled on every poet's pad.
Through it all we keep in mind
what we, every one, know is fact:
that what we seek is really Sex
and Love's just one means to our end.

CONQUERING LOVE

With hope my single ideology, innocence my only weapon,
I rose out of the nursery and went to conquer Love.
I passed all the girls in cellophane, said No to the ones in
bows.
No purpose found I in frivolity: I was out to conquer
Love.

And Love was a Virgin in a Pershing tank, a saint in
burnished chain mail.
And I was Bubba in a pickup truck, an Eskimo in
underwear.
Still, no purpose found I in frivolity. I was out to conquer
Love.

So: I fell on Love with my Weakness, and I fell on Love
with my Hope,
Fell on Love with my Purpose — was all-out to conquer
Love.
But my belief blunted to memory, and my arms were
battered to guile.
I fell back into my hatchery – I was out, oh! conquered by
Love.

'Cause Love's a Virgin in a Sherman tank, Guan Yin in a
steel nuptial veil.
I was a hick in a beat-up truck, an Eskimo exposed to the
bare.
Though I found no purpose in frivolity, I was downed,
conquered by Love.

And so now I pass my time with cellophane girls, say Yes
to those in bows;
manservant of this world I found, not one to conquer
Love.
But sometimes fondly I remember the days before I
learned my craft
When, once in my hopes and my weakness. I had set out
to conquer Love.

LOVES I BEAR TO YOU

Addressing my all-girls class in Seoul
(a sea of knees and eyes) –
just whom do I cast my verbal net unto?
Miss J in her vast lostness of late adolescence
The mirthlessness of Miss O's mercenary matrimonialism
The practiced spontaneity of Miss U's blushes
Miss E's patient burden of passionate virtue
The ancient futures of grown middle school dreams

And then,
in midOthello,
the lights go

out

and in the sudden night
all that I can make out
are the pale fluorescent coral
of fingertips,

lips…

HIGH COUP

O moon, so distant…
I'm not smokin' in Tokyo,
my poem will not fire.

"Revolution bursts
sunlight on stained stainless steel:
your yolk colored hair."

Night's vaunted Shakespeare:
just flaccid Little Willie,
cold to geisha stars.

"Nest raw hair – egg's eye
blue – honeyed limbs; trunk hugging
bear cub Me: climbing."

Sake enflames verse
(you say), arouses rhythm,
kindles rhymes sublime –

mine (old drunken whore)
fires up unsuccessfully,
sucks relentlessly,

till we fall asleep.
And Basho a monk remains,
red raw poem limp, still.

(AND) PURPLE PROSE

The raw sources of a pipefitter's dream
are simple: nuts & nipples & couplings & screws.
And I'm just a poet in search of a muse,
just a sea-starved seaman in need of a cruise.
A poet needs a muse to sweeten his songs,
so won't you play sugar if I play tongue?
Let me lap you up like a cup of cream.
Slyly she replied, *Silver.*

I own my own eye. I'm here to hear rhymes.
But actors need prompters to feed them their cues.
For rams to have lambs they first must have ewes.
Even sticks of dynamite require a fuse.
For to fill my verse up, rim, barrel, and bung,
let me borrow your breath to stuff my lungs.
I don't want my songs to outsilence mimes.
But slow she answered me, *Orange.*

Silver she handed me — poets need gold.
And orange you gave me; it won't balance my blues.
It's like finding the *Times* with ads but no news
or going to church to worship the pews.
Poet needs muse to keep his thoughts young.
The muse is the clothesline on which are hung
poet's pants & fancies before they get cold.
O my silent unrhymed diamond...

SAMIZDAT

[inspired by Solzhenitsyn's *Gulag Archipelago*]

Writer's craft: manacled to conviction
    like any zek to his sentence,
      like a blatnoi to a pen
: assaults its own position
: like a gaybist missionary, assassinates its friends

: like any other virgin—
just another bloody period,
and another conception ends.

YOUR BODY TELLS THE HIGHWAYMAN

If prose is just a page running across your face,
poetry is the line lying between your thighs.

Your body tells the highwayman's short story life:
The drama of poems at the point of conception,
but just one more hackneyed form in execution.

LIFE/SENTENCE

 key in the cake—
(in music, truth hid?)

oh,

the poet's prison is
the rhythm of his
poem
              starved,
              scarred—
he makes his

break

CONFESSIONS

Everyone's a politician,
everyone's a journalist.
And none of us has inhibitions
when it comes to tales to twist.

I went to see my physician
in her office inside my tomb.
For practice, she writes out prescriptions
just to kill the kids in their wombs.

My preacher makes his confession
to the girls who are blonde and young.
He lays on his hands, as his mission,
and exhibits the gifts of his tongues.

Professors write dissertations
in order to hide all the facts.
And if you want real information,
—well, you needn't even ask.

At open mike, that thin coed
that said she hungered for new verse,
("You I'll fill," said I, "your poet.")
starves though swallowed Complete Works.

Was Jesus tacked to an easel
so Romans could paint him later?
They staged all the acts of apostles
just to build wings for their theaters.

And everyone had truth to twist
till they convinced me I was cured.
But when I asked, my psychiatrist
sneered. "Why, no, I'm not even bored!"

"The Many Loves of Duane Vorhees" is devoted to the many aspects of romantic (and sometimes anti-romantic) relationships, from start-ups to breakups and unrequited situations in between, from youthful idealism to cynical manipulation to rediscovered vitality. This book represents the early stages of that evolution.

www.ingramcontent.com/pod-product-compliance
Lightning Source LLC
Chambersburg PA
CBHW030517130626
46549CB00007B/3035